Design: Jill Coote
Recipe Photography: Peter Barry
Recipe styling: Jacqueline Bellefontaine,
Bridgeen Deery and Wendy Devenish
Jacket and Illustration Artwork: Jane Winton,
courtesy of Bernard Thornton Artists, London
Introduced and compiled by Laura Potts
Edited by Josephine Bacon

Published by
CHARTWELL BOOKS, INC.
A Division of **BOOK SALES, INC.**
110 Enterprise Avenue
Secaucus, New Jersey 07094
CLB 3354
© 1993 CLB Publishing,
Godalming, Surrey, England
Printed and bound in Singapore
ISBN 1-55521-983-7

THE LITTLE BOOK ·OF·

Chinese

RECIPES

The perfect introduction to one of the world's oldest and most respected culinary traditions.

CHARTWELL BOOKS, INC.

Introduction

The Chinese, like the French, are a nation of food lovers, and the preparation and enjoyment of food plays a central part in their way of life. The Chinese culinary tradition, one of the oldest in the world, now enjoys an almost unprecedented popularity in the West.

Stir-frying is the most commonly used technique in Chinese cookery and is one with which many people are familiar. This method of cooking, though not difficult to master, is a skill and a few simple rules need to be followed in order to get the best results.

Successful stir-fry dishes rely, in large part, on careful preparation. By chopping or shredding ingredients, a greater surface area is created, which in turn reduces the amount of cooking time required. Care should be taken to ensure that each of the ingredients is cut to roughly the same size. As stir-frying will often take just a few minutes, it is vital to have all the ingredients pre-prepared and the necessary sauces to hand. This helps to avoid last-minute panic, and so helps prevent over-cooking.

Secondly, because stir-frying is so quick and uses such a direct source of heat, it is important to use only the finest ingredients. Texture and taste are fundamental to good Chinese cookery and poor quality ingredients cannot be successfully "hidden." This general rule applies to all ingredients in a recipe, but is particularly important when choosing cuts of meat. Although marinades usually

act as a tenderizer, they cannot perform miracles. Cheap cuts, which need long, slow cooking to break down the tissues, will remain tough if they are stir-fried. In traditional Chinese cookery, meat or fish are used in small amounts, but are used to maximum effect. This emphasis on quality rather than quantity means that the best cuts can be bought while still keeping the overall cost of the dish quite low.

Stir-fry dishes can be cooked in an ordinary skillet, but better results will usually be achieved in a wok. Its gently sloping sides retain the heat far more effectively than a conventional skillet while providing a larger surface area on which to cook the food. When cooking, the wok should be heated, and then the temperature reduced before adding the oil. If the wok is too hot the oil will burn, giving a charred, oily taste to the food. The heat should be progressively raised for the addition of other ingredients, unless otherwise specified in the recipe.

The recipes in this book cover a broad cross-section of Chinese stir-fry dishes and suggest ideas for the rice or noodle dishes to serve with them. The step-by-step recipes are easy to follow and provide the perfect introduction to one of world's oldest and most respected culinary traditions, helping you to recreate the tastes of authentic Chinese cuisine in your own home.

Wonton Soup

SERVES 6-8

The recipe for this classic Chinese soup uses ready-made wonton wrappers.

PREPARATION: 25-30 mins
COOKING: 5-10 mins

20-24 wonton wrappers
2 tbsps chopped Chinese parsley (cilantro)
⅔ cup finely ground chicken or lean pork
3 green onions (scallions), finely chopped
1-inch piece fresh ginger, peeled and grated
1 egg, lightly beaten
3 pints chicken broth
1 tbsp dark soy sauce
Dash sesame oil
Salt and pepper
Chinese parsley or watercress for garnish

Step 3 Fold over the tops and press firmly with the fingers to seal.

Step 2 Place a spoonful of filling on half of each wrapper

1. Place all the wonton wrappers on a large, flat surface. Mix together the chicken or pork, chopped parsley, green onions, and ginger. Brush the edges of the wrappers lightly with beaten egg.

2. Place a small mound of mixture on one half of the wrappers and fold the other half over the top to form a triangle.

3. Press with the fingers to seal the edges well.

4. Bring the broth to the boil in a large saucepan. Add the filled wontons and simmer 5-10 minutes or until they float to the surface. Add remaining ingredients to the soup and garnish.

Spiced Fried Soup

SERVES 4

A delicious, nutritious soup which is a meal in itself.

PREPARATION: 20 mins
COOKING: 20-25 mins

4-8 tbsps oil
1 clove garlic, peeled but left whole
1 pound chicken breast, skinned, boned, and
    cut into small pieces
1 cake tofu, drained and cut into 1-inch cubes
¼ cup raw cashew nuts
4 shallots, roughly chopped
1 carrot, thinly sliced
¼ cup snowpeas
2 ounces Chinese noodles, soaked 5 minutes in
    hot water and drained thoroughly
3 pints vegetable or chicken broth
Juice of 1 lime
¼ tsp turmeric
2 curry leaves
1 tsp grated fresh ginger
1 tbsp soy sauce
Salt and pepper

---

1. Heat 2 tbsps oil in a wok or large skillet. Add the garlic and cook until brown. Remove from the pan and discard.

2. Add the chicken pieces and cook in the oil, until they begin to brown. Remove and drain well.

Step 2 Stir-fry the chicken pieces in hot oil until they begin to brown.

3. Add a little more oil and cook the tofu until lightly brown. Remove and drain well.

4. Add the cashews and cook, stirring constantly until toasted. Remove and drain well.

5. Add a little more oil and fry the shallots and carrots until lightly browned. Stir in the snowpeas and cook 1 minute. Remove from the pan and drain.

6. Heat the remaining oil until it is very hot. Add the noodles and cook quickly until brown on one side. Turn over and brown the other side.

7. Lower the heat and pour in the broth. Stir in the remaining ingredients. Cover and simmer gently for 10 minutes, stirring occasionally.

8. Add the fried ingredients and heat through for 5 minutes. Serve immediately.

Barbecued Spareribs

SERVES 4-6

These tasty spare ribs can be served either as a starter or as part of a larger meal.

PREPARATION: 45 mins, plus 1 hr to marinate the ribs. 4 hrs to soak the green onion garnish
COOKING: 1 hr

4 pounds fresh spare ribs
3 tbsps dark soy sauce
6 tbsps hoisin sauce
2 tbsps dry sherry
¼ tsp five-spice powder
1 tbsp brown sugar
4-6 green onions (scallions) for garnish

1. Trim the root ends and the dark green tops from the green onions.

2. Cut both ends into thin strips, leaving about ½ inch in the middle uncut.

Step 2 Cut both ends of the green onions into thin strips, leaving the middle whole.

Step 3 Place in ice water and leave to stand 4 hours or overnight until the ends curl.

3. Place in ice water for several hours or overnight for the ends to curl up.

4. Cut the spareribs into one-inch pieces. Mix all the remaining ingredients together, pour over the ribs, and stir to coat evenly. Allow to stand 1 hour.

5. Put the sparerib pieces on a rack in a roasting pan containing 2½ cups water and cook in a preheated 350°F oven 30 minutes. Add more hot water to the pan while cooking, if necessary.

6. Turn the ribs over and brush with the remaining sauce. Cook 30 minutes longer, or until tender. Serve garnished with the green onion brushes.

Quick Fried Shrimp

SERVES 4-6

This easy-to-cook recipe can be prepared with either raw or cooked shrimp.

PREPARATION: 30 mins for the shrimp to
marinate
COOKING: 2 mins

---

2 pounds cooked shrimp in their shells
2 cloves garlic, crushed
1-inch piece fresh ginger root, finely chopped
1 tbsp chopped fresh Chinese parsley (cilantro)
3 tbsps oil
1 tbsp rice wine or dry sherry
1½ tbsps light soy sauce
Chopped green onions (scallions) to garnish

---

1. Shell the shrimp except for the very tail
ends. Place the shrimp in a bowl with the
remaining ingredients, except for the garnish,
and leave to marinate 30 minutes.

2. Heat the wok and add the shrimp and the
marinade. Stir-fry briefly to heat the cooked
shrimp.

Step 1
Carefully pull
the head of the
shrimp away
from the body.

3. Chop the onions roughly. Sprinkle over the
shrimp and serve immediately.

Step 2 Peel the
shells from the
shrimp,
leaving only
the tail ends.

Shrimp Egg Fried Rice

SERVES 6

This rice dish is substantial enough to eat as a meal on its own

PREPARATION: 20 mins
COOKING: 15 mins

---

1 pound long grain rice
2 eggs
½ tsp salt
4 tbsps oil
2 green onions (scallions), chopped
1 large onion, chopped
2 garlic cloves, chopped
½ cup bay shrimp, peeled
½ cup shelled peas
2 tbsps dark soy sauce

---

1. Wash the rice thoroughly and put it in a saucepan. Add water to come 1 inch above the top of the rice.

Step 3 Rinse the rice in cold water and separate the grains with a fork.

Step 4 Cook the eggs with the onions gently, until set and softly scrambled.

2. Bring the rice to the boil, stir once, then reduce the heat. Cover and simmer until the liquid has been absorbed, about 20 minutes.

3. Rinse the rice in cold water and separate the grains with a fork.

4. Beat the eggs with a pinch of salt. Heat 1 tablespoon of the oil in a wok and cook the green onions and the onion until soft. Add the egg and stir gently, until the mixture is set. Remove the egg mixture and set it aside.

5. Heat a further tablespoon of the oil and fry the garlic, shrimp, and peas 2 minutes. Remove and set aside.

6. Heat the remaining oil in the wok and stir in the rice and salt. Stir-fry, to heat the rice through, then add the egg and the shrimp mixtures, and the soy sauce. Serve immediately.

Fried Rice

SERVES 6-8

The traditional Chinese accompaniment to stir-fried dishes.

Preparation: 30 mins
Cooking: 4 mins

4 cups cooked rice, well drained and dried
3 tbsps oil
1 egg, beaten
1 tbsp soy sauce
½ cup cooked peas
2 green onions (scallions), thinly sliced
Dash sesame oil
Salt and pepper

Step 2 Stir to coat the rice with egg, and toss mixture over heat to separate grains of rice.

Step 2 Add rice and peas on top of egg mixture.

1. Heat a wok and add the oil. Pour in the egg and soy sauce and cook until just beginning to set.

2. Add the rice and peas and stir to coat with the egg mixture. Allow to cook about 3 minutes, stirring continuously. Add seasoning and sesame oil.

3. Spoon into a serving dish and sprinkle with the green onions.

Stir-Fry Noodles

SERVES 4

This enticing recipe is easy to prepare and makes an ideal supper dish.

PREPARATION: 20 mins
COOKING: 15 mins

---

1 × 8-ounce package fine egg noodles
4 tbsps peanut oil
1 onion, finely chopped
2 cloves garlic, crushed
1 green chili, seeded and finely sliced
1 tsp chili paste
4 ounces pork, finely sliced
2 sticks of celery, sliced
¼ small cabbage, finely shredded
1 tbsp light soy sauce
4 ounces shrimp, shelled and deveined
Salt and pepper

Step 4 Stir-fry the pork, celery, and cabbage with the onion mixture for 3 minutes, or until the pork is cooked through.

Step 1 Soak the noodles in hot water 5 minutes, until they are soft. Rinse in cold water and drain thoroughly in a colander.

1. Soak the noodles in hot water for 5 minutes, until they are soft. Rinse in cold water and drain thoroughly in a colander.

2. Heat the oil in a wok and stir-fry the onion, garlic, and chili, until the onion is soft and just golden brown.

3. Add the chili paste and stir well.

4. Add the pork, celery, and cabbage, and stir-fry about 3 minutes, or until the pork is cooked through. Season to taste.

5. Stir in the soy sauce, noodles, and shrimp, tossing the mixture together thoroughly and heating through before serving.

Sweet-and-Sour Pork

SERVES 2-4

This popular dish originated in Canton.

PREPARATION: 15 mins
COOKING: 15 mins

---

1 cup all-purpose flour
4 tbsps cornstarch
1½ tsps baking powder
Pinch salt
1 tbsp oil
Water
8 ounces pork fillet, cut into ½-inch cubes
1 onion, sliced
1 green bell pepper, seeded, cored, and sliced
1 small can pineapple chunks, juice reserved
Oil for frying

Sweet-and-Sour Sauce
2 tbsps cornstarch
½ cup light brown sugar
Pinch salt
½ cup cider vinegar or rice vinegar
1 clove garlic, crushed
1 tsp root ginger, grated
6 tbsps tomato ketchup
6 tbsps pineapple juice reserved from the can

---

1. Sift the flour, cornstarch, baking powder, and salt into a bowl. Add the oil and enough water to make a thick, smooth batter. Beat until smooth.

Step 2 Dip the pork cubes into the batter and then drop into hot oil.

2. Heat enough oil in a wok to deep-fry the pork. Dip the pork cubes into the batter and drop into the hot oil. Fry 4-5 pieces of pork at a time and remove them with a slotted spoon to paper towels. Continue until all the pork is fried.

3. Pour off most of the oil from the wok and add the sliced onion, pepper, and pineapple. Cook over high heat for 1-2 minutes. Remove and set aside.

4. Mix all the sauce ingredients together and pour into the wok. Bring slowly to the boil, stirring continuously until thickened. Allow to simmer about 1-2 minutes or until completely clear.

5. Add the vegetables, pineapple, and pork to the sauce and stir well. Reheat for 1-2 minutes and serve immediately.

Pork Chow Mein

SERVES 4

Sliced beef or chicken can also be used in this classic Chinese dish.

PREPARATION: 20 mins
COOKING: 20 mins

---

1 × 10-ounce package egg noodles
1 tbsp Chinese wine or dry sherry
1 tbsp light soy sauce
1 tsp sugar
1 pound pork fillet, thinly sliced
3 tbsps oil
1 tsp grated root ginger
1 stick celery, sliced diagonally
1 leek, finely sliced
1 red bell pepper, cored, seeded, sliced
1 small can bamboo shoots, sliced
⅔ cup broth
2 tbsps peas
1 tsp cornstarch
1 tbsp water
Salt and pepper

---

1. Soak the noodles in hot water 5 minutes, then rinse in cold water and drain thoroughly.

2. Combine the wine, soy sauce, and sugar in a large bowl. Add the pork, mix well, and leave to marinate for 15 minutes.

3. Heat the oil in a large wok, and add the ginger, celery, and leek. Stir-fry 2 minutes.

4. Add the red pepper and bamboo shoots and stir-fry a further 2 minutes.

Step 4 Add the red pepper and bamboo shoots and stir-fry a further 2 minutes.

5. Remove the vegetables from the wok. Increase the heat and add the pork, reserving the marinade. Stir-fry 4 minutes, or until cooked through.

6. Return the vegetables to the wok, mixing with the pork. Add the broth gradually, stirring well.

7. Add the peas and cook 2 minutes.

8. Mix the cornstarch with the water, add to the marinade, and stir in well.

9. Stir the marinade sauce into the vegetables and pork in the wok. Mix well until the sauce is thickened and smooth. Add the noodles, and stir everything together thoroughly until the mixture has heated through.

10. Season to taste and simmer 3 minutes before serving.

Stir-Fried Calves' Liver with Bell Peppers and Carrots

SERVES 4

Quick stir-frying ensures that the calves' liver remains pink and tender inside.

PREPARATION: 15-20 mins
COOKING: 10-12 mins

2 tbsps oil
1 onion, thinly sliced
1 clove garlic, finely sliced
1½ pounds calves' liver, cut into thin strips
2 tbsps seasoned wholewheat flour
4 tbsps dry sherry or Chinese rice wine
140ml/¼ pint water or vegetable broth
1 green bell pepper, seeded, and cut into strips
3 large carrots, cut into strips
Salt and pepper
½ cup beansprouts

Step 5 Stir in the beansprouts and heat through about 1 minute, until they are warm, but still crunchy.

Step 2 Roll the strips of calves' liver in the seasoned flour, until they are evenly coated.

1. Heat the oil in a wok and stir-fry the onion and garlic 3 minutes.

2. Roll the strips of liver in the seasoned flour and add to the wok, along with the onion. Stir-fry quickly, until the liver is sealed on the outside, but is still pink in the center.

3. Stir in the sherry or rice wine and bring to a rapid boil. Add the water, or broth, along with the green pepper, carrots, and seasoning.

4. Stir-fry the liver in the sauce 3 minutes, over a high heat.

5. Add the beansprouts to the wok and stir-fry 1 minute, then serve.

Shredded Beef with Vegetables

SERVES 4

Red and green chili peppers give an extra kick to this tasty stir-fry

PREPARATION: 15 mins
COOKING: 10 mins

8 ounces lean beef, cut into thin strips
½ tsp salt
4 tbsps vegetable oil
1 red and 1 green chili pepper, seeded and
  sliced into strips
1 tsp vinegar
1 stick celery, cut into thin strips
2 carrots, cut into thin strips
1 leek, white part only, sliced into thin strips
2 cloves garlic, finely chopped
1 tbsp light soy sauce
1 tbsp dark soy sauce
2 tsps Chinese wine or dry sherry
1 tsp superfine sugar
½ tsp freshly ground black pepper

1. Put the strips of beef into a large bowl and sprinkle with the salt. Rub the salt into the meat and allow to stand 5 minutes.

2. Heat 1 tbsp of the oil in a large wok. When the oil begins to smoke, reduce the heat and stir in the beef and the chilies. Stir-fry 4-5 minutes.

3. Add the remaining oil and continue stir-frying the beef, until it turns crispy.

Step 1 Rub the salt well into the sliced beef and leave to stand.

4. Add the vinegar and stir until it evaporates, then add the celery, carrots, leek, and garlic. Stir-fry 2 minutes.

5. Mix together the soy sauces, wine or sherry, sugar, and pepper. Pour this mixture over the beef and cook 2 minutes. Serve immediately.

Step 5 Pour in the soy sauce mixture and stir-fry rapidly about 2 minutes, making sure that the beef and vegetables are well coated.

Spiced Beef

SERVES 4

Ground star anise and fennel bring a hint of licorice to this fragrant, spicy stir-fry.

PREPARATION: 30 mins
COOKING: 5-6 mins

---

1 pound fillet of beef
1 tsp soft brown sugar
2-3 star anise, ground
½ tsp ground fennel
1 tbsp dark soy sauce
1-inch piece fresh root ginger, grated
½ tsp salt
2 tbsps oil
6 green onions (scallions), sliced
1 tbsp light soy sauce
½ tsp freshly ground black pepper

---

1. Cut the beef into thin strips 1-inch long, cutting across the grain of the meat.

2. Mix the sugar, spices, and dark soy sauce in a bowl.

Step 5 Stir-fry the beef with the green onions 4 minutes.

3. Add the beef, ginger, and salt and stir well to coat evenly. Cover and allow to stand 20 minutes.

4. Heat the oil in a wok and stir-fry the onions 1 minute.

5. Add the beef and fry, stirring constantly, 4 minutes, or until the meat is well browned.

6. Stir in the light soy sauce and black pepper and cook gently for a further 1 minute.

Beef with Broccoli

SERVES 2-3

Cutting the meat across the grain ensures that it will be tender and will cook quickly.

PREPARATION: 25 mins
COOKING: 4 mins

---

1 pound rump steak, partially frozen
4 tbsps dark soy sauce
1 tbsp cornstarch
1 tbsp rice wine or dry sherry
1 tsp sugar
1 cup fresh broccoli
6 tbsps oil
1-inch piece ginger, peeled and shredded
Salt and pepper

---

1. Trim any fat from the meat and cut into very thin strips across the grain.

Step 1 Use partially frozen meat and slice it thinly across the grain.

Step 3 Cut the broccoli stalks in thin diagonal slices.

2. Combine the meat with the soy sauce, cornstarch, sherry, and sugar. Stir well and leave long enough for the meat to completely defrost.

3. Cut the broccoli into even-sized flowerets. Peel the stalks of the broccoli and cut into thin, diagonal slices.

4. Heat 2 tbsps of the oil in a wok. Add the broccoli and sprinkle with salt. Stir-fry until the broccoli is dark green. Do not cook longer than 2 minutes. Remove from the wok and set aside.

5. Place the remaining oil in the wok, and add the ginger and beef. Stir-fry about 2 minutes. Return the broccoli to the pan and mix well. Heat through for 30 seconds then serve.

Chicken with Walnuts and Celery

SERVES 4

Oyster sauce lends a subtle, slightly salty taste to this Cantonese dish.

PREPARATION: 20 mins
COOKING: 8 mins

8 ounces skinned and boned chicken, cut into
    1-inch pieces
2 tsps soy sauce
2 tsps brandy
1 tsp cornstarch
Salt and pepper
2 tbsps oil
1 garlic clove, left whole
½ cup walnut halves
3 sticks celery, cut in diagonal slices
⅔ cup chicken broth
2 tsps oyster sauce

Step 3 Add the walnuts to the wok and cook until they are crisp.

Step 4 Use a large, sharp knife to cut the celery on the diagonal into thin slices.

1. Combine the chicken with the soy sauce, brandy, cornstarch, salt, and pepper.

2. Heat a wok and add the oil and garlic. Cook the garlic about 1 minute to flavor the oil, then remove.

3. Add the chicken in two batches. Stir-fry quickly without allowing the chicken to brown. Remove the chicken and add the walnuts to the wok. Cook about 2 minutes until they are slightly brown.

4. Slice the celery, add to the wok and cook 1 minute. Add the oyster sauce and broth and bring to the boil. When boiling, return the chicken to the pan and stir well. Serve immediately.

Singapore Fish

SERVES 6

The cuisine of Singapore was much influenced by that of China. In turn, the Chinese brought ingredients like curry powder into their own cuisine.

PREPARATION: 25 mins
COOKING: 10 mins

---

1 pound white fish fillets
1 egg white
1 tbsp cornstarch
2 tsps white wine
Salt and pepper
Oil for frying
1 large onion, coarsely chopped
1 tbsp mild curry powder
1 small can pineapple chunks, drained, juice
    reserved
1 small can mandarin orange segments,
    drained, juice reserved
1 small can sliced water chestnuts, drained
1 tbsp cornstarch
Juice of 1 lime
2 tsps sugar (optional)
Pinch salt and pepper

---

1. Starting at the tail end of the fillets, skin them using a sharp knife.

2. Slide the knife back and forth along the length of each fillet, pushing the fish flesh along as you go.

3. Cut the fish into even-sized pieces, about 2 inches.

Step 2 Hold filleting knife at a slight angle and slide knife along length of fillet in a sawing motion.

4. Mix together the egg white, cornstarch, wine, salt, and pepper. Place the fish in the mixture and leave to stand while heating the oil.

5. When the oil is hot, fry a few pieces of fish at a time until golden-brown and crisp. Remove the fish to paper towels to drain once it is cooked.

6. Remove all but 1 tbsp of the oil from the wok, and add the onion. Stir-fry 1-2 minutes and add the curry powder. Cook a further 1-2 minutes. Add the juice from the canned fruit and bring to the boil.

7. Combine the cornstarch and lime juice and add a spoonful of the boiling fruit juice. Return the mixture to the wok and cook until thickened. Taste and add sugar if desired. Add the fruit, water chestnuts, and fried fish to the wok and stir to coat. Heat through 1 minute and serve immediately.

Kung Pao Shrimp with Cashew Nuts

SERVES 6

This easy dish combines many different textures and tastes.

PREPARATION: 20 mins
COOKING: 3 mins

½ tsp chopped fresh ginger root
1 tsp chopped garlic
1½ tbsps cornstarch
¼ tsp baking soda
Salt and pepper
¼ tsp sugar
1 pound raw shrimp
4 tbsps oil
1 small onion, diced
1 large or 2 small zucchini, coarsely chopped
1 small red bell pepper, coarsely chopped
½ cup cashew nuts

Sauce
¾ cup chicken broth
1 tbsp cornstarch
2 tsps chili sauce
2 tsps bean paste (optional)
2 tsps sesame oil
1 tbsp dry sherry or rice wine

---

1. Mix together the ginger, garlic, cornstarch, baking soda, salt, pepper, and sugar.

2. If the shrimp are unpeeled, peel and devein them. If large, cut in half. Place in the dry ingredients and leave to stand 20 minutes.

Step 4 To dice the zucchini quickly, top and tail, and cut into strips.

3. Heat the oil in a wok and when hot add the shrimp. Stir-fry about 20 seconds, or just until the shrimp turn color. Transfer to a plate.

4. Add the onion to the same oil and cook about 1 minute. Add the zucchini and red pepper and cook about 30 seconds.

5. Mix the sauce ingredients together and add to the wok. Cook, stirring constantly, until the sauce is thickened. Add the shrimp and the cashew nuts and heat through.

Step 4 Cut the strips across with a large sharp knife.

Special Mixed Vegetables

SERVES 4

This dish illustrates the basic stir-frying technique for vegetables.

PREPARATION: 25 mins
COOKING: 3 mins

1 tbsp oil
1 clove garlic, crushed
1-inch piece root ginger, sliced
4 Chinese (Nappa) cabbage leaves, shredded
½ cup thinly sliced flat mushrooms
½ cup bamboo shoots, sliced
3 sticks celery, diagonally sliced
½ cup baby corn, cut in half if large
1 small red bell pepper, thinly sliced
½ cup bean sprouts
2 tbsps light soy sauce
Dash sesame oil
Salt and pepper
3 tomatoes, peeled, seeded, and quartered

Step Place in cold water to stop the cooking. The skin will then peel away easily.

Step 2 To peel the tomatoes, place them first in a pan of boiling water 5 seconds. Tomatoes that are very ripe need less time.

1. Heat the oil in a wok and add the ingredients in the order given, reserving the tomatoes until last.

2. To make it easier to peel the tomatoes, remove the stems and place in boiling water 5 seconds.

3. Remove from the boiling water and place in a bowl of cold water. This will make the skin easier to remove. Cut out the core end.

4. Cut the tomatoes in half and then in quarters and remove the seeds.

5. Cook the vegetables about 2 minutes. Stir in the soy sauce and sesame oil, and add the tomatoes. Heat through 30 seconds and serve immediately.

Stir-Fry Tofu Salad

SERVES 4-6

Ideal for vegetarians, but so delicious that it will be enjoyed by everyone.

PREPARATION: 25 mins
COOKING: 2-4 mins

1 cake tofu
½ cup snowpeas
½ cup mushrooms
2 carrots, peeled
2 sticks celery
½ cup broccoli flowerets
⅔ cup oil
3 tbsps lemon juice
2 tsps honey
1 tsp grated fresh ginger root
3 tbsps soy sauce
Dash of sesame oil
4 green onions (scallions)
2 tbsps unsalted roasted peanuts
½ cup beansprouts
½ head Chinese (Nappa) cabbage

1. Drain the tofu well and press gently to remove any excess moisture. Cut into cubes.

2. Trim the tops and tails from the snowpeas.

3. Thinly slice the mushrooms with a sharp knife.

4. Cut the carrots and celery into thin slices.

5. Trim the green onions and slice them.

6. Heat 2 tbsps of the vegetable oil in a wok.

Step 4 Cut the vegetables with your knife at an angle to produce diagonal pieces.

Stir in the snowpeas, mushrooms, celery, carrots, and broccoli, and cook 2 minutes, stirring constantly.

7. Remove the vegetables from the wok and set them aside to cool.

8. Put the remaining oil into a small bowl and whisk in the lemon juice, honey, ginger, soy sauce, and sesame oil.

9. Stir the green onions, peanuts, and beansprouts into the cooled vegetables.

10. Mix the dressing into the vegetables, then add the tofu, tossing it carefully so that it does not break up.

11. Shred the Chinese cabbage and arrange it on a serving platter. Pile the salad ingredients over the top and serve well chilled.

Index

Appetizers:
  Barbecued Spareribs 12
  Spiced Fried Soup 10
  Wonton Soup 8
Barbecued Spareribs 12
Beef with Broccoli 32
Chicken with Walnuts and Celery 34
Fish and Seafood:
  Kung Pao Shrimp with Cashew Nuts 38
  Quick Fried Shrimp 14
  Singapore Fish 36
  Stir-Fry Noodles 20
  Fried Rice 18
Kung Pao Shrimp with Cashew Nuts 38
Meat:
  Beef with Broccoli 32
  Pork Chow Mein 24
  Shredded Beef with Vegetables 28
  Spiced Beef 30
  Stir-Fried Calves' Liver with Peppers
    and Carrots 26
  Sweet-and-Sour Pork 22
Noodles:

  Stir-Fry Noodles 20
Pork Chow Mein 24
Poultry:
  Chicken with Walnuts and Celery 34
Quick Fried Shrimp 14
Shrimp Egg Fried Rice 16
Rice Dishes:
  Fried Rice 18
  Shrimp Egg Fried Rice 16
Shredded Beef with Vegetables 28
Singapore Fish 36
Special Mixed Vegetables 40
Spiced Beef 30
Spiced Fried Soup 10
Stir-Fried Calves' Liver with Peppers and
  Carrots 26
Stir-Fry Noodles 20
Stir-Fry Tofu Salad 42
Sweet-and-Sour Pork 22
Vegetarian:
  Special Mixed Vegetables 40
  Stir-Fry Tofu Salad 42
Wonton Soup 8

Stir-Fried Calves' Liver with Peppers and Carrots